Frederick Douglass
FIGHTS FOR FREEDOM

Frederick Douglass
FIGHTS FOR FREEDOM
Margaret Davidson

SCHOLASTIC INC.
New York Toronto London Auckland Sydney

Almost all the pictures in this book were made during the time Frederick Douglass lived. Some are photographs, and some were drawn by artists.

p. 6: Library of Congress; p. 9: Baltimore Historical Society, photo by Ann Grifalconi; p. 14: courtesy Penn Community Center; p. 21: New York Public Library Picture Collection; p. 25: Library of Congress; p. 27: Library of Congress; p. 37: Library of Congress; p. 42: New York Public Library Picture Collection; p. 54: Library of Congress; p. 58: New York Public Library Picture Collection; p. 64: National Park Service, photo by Ann Grifalconi; p. 74: Ann Grifalconi; p. 78: Culver Pictures; p. 80: Ann Grifalconi.

ISBN 0–590–42218–9

Text copyright © 1968 by Margaret Davidson. Illustrations copyright © 1968 by Scholastic Books, Inc. All rights reserved. Published by Scholastic Inc.

12 11 10 9 8 7 6 5   1 2 3 4/9

To
Martin Luther King, Jr.
and
Robert Francis Kennedy

Frederick Douglass was born in 1817 and died in 1895. He was about 50 years old when this photograph was taken.

The Happy Years

"GRANDMA, when was I born?"

"Why, Frederick, you know that," said his grandmother. "You were born about six years ago."

But Frederick didn't want to know *about* when he was born. He wanted to know *exactly*. "When was my birthday?" he asked.

"Why do you want to know?"

"Because everyone else knows. Edward knows and Philip knows, and Mr. Lee knows, and . . ."

"That's different," Grandmother Bailey said shortly. "They're white."

Frederick Douglass was a famous man. He was respected. Sometimes he was feared, for he had a very sharp tongue. He could fight for his people.

Frederick Douglass fought for laws that would protect blacks, for better schools, for better jobs. And he grew more and more famous. His name was honored around the world.

But in the beginning...

FLAMING
ABOLITION SPEECH
DELIVERED BY THE RUNAWAY SLAVE,
FREDERICK DOUGLASS,
At the Anniversary of the American Anti-Slavery Society,
IN THE TABERNACLE, NEW YORK, MAY 11, 1847.

The following Report will show to Marylanders, how a runaway slave talks, when he reaches the Abolition regions of the country. This presumptive negro was even present at the London World's Temperance Convention, last year; and in spite of all the efforts of the American Delegates to prevent it, he palmed off his Abolition bombast upon an audience of 7000 persons! Of this high-handed measure he now makes his boast in New-York, one of the hot-beds of Abolitionism. The Report is given exactly as published in the New-York Tribune. The reader will make his own comments.

"Mr. Douglass was introduced to the audience by Wm. Lloyd Garrison, Esq., President of the American Anti-Slavery Society, and, upon taking the platform, was greeted with enthusiastic and long-continued applause by the vast concourse which filled the spacious Tabernacle to overflowing. As soon as the audience became silent, Mr. D. with, at first, a slight degree of embarrassment, addressed them as follows:

I am very glad to be here. I am very glad to be present at this Anniversary—glad again to mingle my voice with those with whom I have stood identified, with those with whom I have labored, for the last seven ... ose of undoing the burdens of my brethren, and has

Who Was Frederick Douglass?

"HE IS MY FRIEND," Abraham Lincoln said about Frederick Douglass. Frederick Douglass was one of the most famous men in America. He had many famous friends — Presidents of the United States and judges and teachers, poets and writers and artists.

Why was he so famous? Why did people respect him so much?

Frederick Douglass *cared* about other people. He was born a slave. He was owned like a horse or a pig or a cow. When he was twenty-one he ran away to the northern states. There he could live as a free man. But Frederick Douglass could not forget the millions of men and women and children who were slaves in the South.

"How can I help?" he asked himself. He was only a poor runaway slave himself.

Frederick Douglass found ways to help. He traveled from town to town telling people about slavery. Large crowds came to hear him speak. He wrote the story of his life as a slave. Many people read it — and knew how it *felt* to be owned like a horse or a pig or a cow. He started a newspaper where blacks could speak for themselves. He helped slaves escape on the Underground Railroad.

In 1861 the Civil War began. When it was over, the slaves were freed at last. But their troubles were not over. In many places blacks had to do work that no one else wanted to do. They had to live in poor sections of town. Their children had to go to tumble-down schools — or not go to school at all. Who could fight for their rights?

"Maybe I could ask someone . . ."

His grandmother was sewing. Now she put down her sewing. She leaned forward. "Listen to me, Frederick," she said. "And listen sharp." Her voice was very stern. "You will ask no one. Do you hear? You are a slave, Frederick. Remember that. You are a slave — and slaves don't need birthdays!"

Frederick Augustus Washington Bailey was born in the state of Maryland sometime in February, 1817. He never knew the exact day. For he was born a slave — he was owned by another man. Frederick was owned by a man named Captain Aaron Anthony. The slaves called him "Old Master."

Old Master owned Frederick's mother too. But Frederick hardly remembered her at all. Soon after Frederick was born Old Master sent Frederick's mother away. He sent the baby Frederick to live with Grandmother Bailey.

Grandmother's cabin was only a tumble-down shack in the little town of Tuckahoe. It had no real floor — just the bare earth. It had no windows at all. But to Frederick it was home — because his grandmother was there.

Those were the happy years, the first years with Grandmother Bailey. Frederick wanted them to go on forever. But he knew they would not. He knew that Grandmother Bailey only raised children until they were old enough to work. Then they were sent back to Old Master again.

Leave his grandmother? The thought scared Frederick. "Maybe Old Master will forget about me," he thought. "I'm awfully skinny and small."

But he was growing.

Frederick could remember a time when he had not been able to touch the bottom branch of the pine tree beside the cabin — no matter how high he stretched. Now he had to bend his head when he walked under it.

"Maybe if I don't eat so much," Frederick thought, "I'll stop growing." But soon he got hungry. Nothing helped anyway. Time kept passing, and Frederick kept growing. One morning his grandmother called. "Frederick? Where are you? Hurry, child. We're going on a trip."

A trip? Frederick came running. Once he had gone through the woods to Mr. Lee's sawmill. He had been down-river as far as the next farm. But he had never gone on a *real* trip before.

He danced up and down with excitement. His feet kicked up little puffs of dust. He was far too excited to be worried. "Where? Where?" he cried.

But Grandmother just shook her head. "You'll see," was all she would say.

Frederick and his grandmother walked for a long time. The road was dusty and the day was hot. Frederick's feet began to drag. Finally they came to the end of their trip.

Frederick saw a big brick house. Behind the house was a barn and many smaller buildings. Later Frederick learned that these were slave-quarters — where the slaves lived — and storehouses and shops. Fields of corn and tobacco stretched as far as he could see.

Slave-quarters like the ones Frederick lived in

"Where are we, Grandma?" he whispered.

"They call this Big House Farm," she answered.

"Who lives *there?*" Frederick pointed to the brick house.

"Old Master," Grandmother said quietly.

No! Frederick pulled back on his grandmother's hand.

"Let's go home!" he cried.

But Grandmother shook her head. She held Frederick's hand tightly, and kept on walking toward the brick house.

The Life
of a Slave

HIS GRANDMOTHER had gone! She had gone and left Frederick in this place! He was only six years old, and now it was time to begin working as a slave. Frederick knew that the happy years were over.

There were many slaves at Big House Farm. They did many different kinds of work. There was a blacksmith and a shoemaker and a tailor. There were carpenters and weavers and maids and cooks. But most of the slaves were field hands. Their job was to plant and plow and pick the corn and tobacco that was grown at Big House Farm.

Frederick learned very quickly what it meant to be a slave at Big House Farm. It meant sleeping on the floor because he had no bed. It meant shivering in winter because he had no warm clothes to wear. It meant being hungry all the time.

Frederick saw the older slaves working from dawn to dark. He saw them whipped for almost any reason — or no reason at all. And he wondered when *his* turn would come.

Frederick was still too young to work in the fields. He swept the walks in front of Old Master's house. He kept the barnyard clean. He shooed chickens out of the vegetable garden. He drove the cows home at night.

His work wasn't hard. But as time went on Frederick grew more and more unhappy. Often he lay awake at night. And his mind filled with questions. Why was he hungry all the time? Why was he dressed in rags? *Why was he a slave at all?*

"Why am I a slave?" he asked Aunt Katy, the cook. But Aunt Katy was in a bad mood. "Go away," she snapped. "Stop asking fool questions."

"Why am I a slave?" he asked William, the carpenter.

"Because that's the way things are," he said.

"Why am I a slave?" he asked Old Barney, who took care of the horses.

"Because God in Heaven wants it that way," Old Barney said.

Again and again Frederick asked his question. He got many different answers. But none satisfied him. He grew more and more unhappy with his life as a slave.

One day Frederick noticed a bird up in a tree. The bird was singing as if its heart would burst with joy. Suddenly it took to the air. It wheeled over Frederick's head and flew out of sight.

"I bet you sing so pretty because you're free," Frederick whispered.

Then Frederick thought up a new question to ask. He asked a wise old woman who reminded him of his grandmother. "Can I get free if I pray for it?"

The old woman thought for a long time. "Depends how you do it," she said at last. "Some folks pray with their mouths ... Some pray with their hearts ... And some folks pray with their feet. Yes, indeed — some folks pray with their feet."

Frederick didn't understand. Not then. But a few weeks later he heard shouting in the barnyard. He came running. And there was Old Master, yelling at a group of slaves.

"Where are they?" he shouted. "Where have they gone?"

Nobody said a word.

Old Master's face grew redder and redder. "I'll catch them!" he promised. "And when I do I'll beat their hides off!"

Still nobody said anything. Except Frederick.

"What *is* it?" he cried. "What's happening?"

A man standing nearby whispered, "Your Aunt Jennie and Uncle Noah are gone, boy. They have gone and followed that old North Star to freedom."

"What's that?" Frederick cried. "Where?"

"Hush, boy." The man's voice was still soft as wind. But his hand gripped Frederick's shoulder hard. "Do you want to get us all in trouble?"

Frederick shook his head. "But what's happening?" he whispered.

"Your aunt and uncle have escaped," the man said. "They've escaped to the northern states. Don't you understand? *They're free.*"

There was so much Frederick still didn't understand. What was the North Star? Where were these northern states? But one thing was perfectly clear. His Aunt Jennie and Uncle Noah were gone from this place. They were *free*.

So that's what the old woman had meant when she said some people prayed with their feet! Aunt Jennie and Uncle Noah had run away! Frederick stood very still. He shut his eyes tight. And he made a vow — a promise to himself. "I don't know how . . . I don't know when . . . But some day I'm going to get free too!"

Sometimes slaves escaped in boats.

The Biggest Lesson of All

"FREDERICK? Come here."

It was Miss Lucretia, one of Old Master's daughters. She held a letter in her hand. "Go and wash," she said. "And be sure to scrub off all that dirt. My husband's brother has written from Baltimore. He needs a servant to take care of his little boy. I figure you're about eight now — plenty old enough to take some responsibility. So we have decided to send you."

Frederick spent the next three days in the creek scrubbing himself all over. He was leaving Big House Farm! He was leaving Big House Farm! Many years later Frederick Douglass wrote, "Those were three of the happiest days of my life."

Frederick rode off to Baltimore. He looked back only once. Then he faced forward. Forward to what? He didn't know. He didn't care either. Whatever lay ahead — it just *had* to be better than Big House Farm.

And it was. From the beginning Frederick felt at home in Baltimore. He liked its busy, bustling, city ways. But most of all he liked the Aulds — the family he had been sent to serve. They gave him food and clothes and a warm bed to sleep in. And they gave him one thing more — kindness.

Frederick's days were busy with work. He ran errands for Master Hugh Auld.

He helped Miss Sophia — as the master's wife was called — around the house. And he watched over little Tommy, their son. The evenings were the best of all. Often Master Hugh had to go out on business. Then Miss Sophia took a book and read aloud to Frederick.

Frederick loved the sound of her voice. Sometimes he leaned over and looked at the book in her lap. Those strange marks on the pages were words. Frederick knew that. But what did they mean?

Finally he could stand it no longer. "Miss Sophia, I want to read!" Frederick burst out one evening. "Please teach me to read for myself!"

Miss Sophia thought it was a fine idea. Lessons began the next day. Frederick was a fast learner. Before the first week was over he knew all the letters of the alphabet. Then Miss Sophia began to teach him short words.

Miss Sophia teaching Frederick to read

She was very pleased with her pupil. "He's so quick!" she said to her husband one evening. Miss Sophia expected her husband to be pleased too. But he was not.

"What have you done?" he cried. "You must stop at once!"

Why was he so angry? Miss Sophia didn't understand. Her husband explained. His voice was so loud that Frederick — who was in the back of the house — heard. He crept close to the door to listen.

"Are you out of your mind? Don't you know it's against the law to teach a slave to read and write?"

"Why?" Miss Sophia asked.

"He'll get *ideas* out of books. He'll begin to *think*."

Miss Sophia still didn't understand. "What's wrong with that?" she asked.

"Don't you see?" her husband said. "Then he will be unhappy with his life as a slave. Why, he might even find out a way to get free!"

Miss Sophia was not sure she agreed with her husband. But she was a good wife. She said she would stop giving Frederick lessons.

Finally Frederick crept back to bed — but not to sleep. Not that night. His heart was hammering too hard. His mind was exploding with thoughts.

So books were bad for a slave! Learning would help set him free! Miss Sophia had taught Frederick the letters of the alphabet and his first small words. But Frederick knew that Master Hugh had taught him a much bigger lesson that night — learning would help set him free!

He had no pencils or pens or papers or books. He didn't even have a teacher anymore. "But I *will* learn how to read and write," Frederick whispered fiercely. "Somehow!"

This is what Baltimore looked like around the time Frederick lived there and worked for Hugh Auld.

A Slave
for Life

FREDERICK FOUND some pages of a book in the gutter. The pages were wrinkled and spattered with mud. But they were a beginning. There were words on those pages — words to learn. Frederick brushed the mud off. He smoothed the pages out. He took them home to study.

Then Frederick found an old Webster's spelling book. Its cover was torn. Its pages were tattered. But there were words in that book — many more words to learn. So Frederick took the book home too.

He had to be careful. If he were caught, Frederick knew he would be stopped. His precious pile of words would be taken away from him. Sometimes he was sent on an errand. Then he took his spelling book with him. He did the errand as quickly as he could — and used the extra few minutes to study. At night when everyone else was asleep he studied by the light of the moon.

And he learned — but not fast enough. He still needed help. Frederick had an idea. He knew many of the white boys who lived in the neighborhood. They were very poor. Their clothes were not as good as Frederick's. Often they didn't have enough to eat. But they could go to school. They already knew how to read and write. Now Frederick got them to teach him.

Their names were Bill, Gus, Joe, and Charley. Sometimes Frederick paid for his lesson with a piece of bread spread thick with butter. Sometimes the boys gave him a lesson for free. But sometimes the boys were not interested in giving lessons at all — not even for bread and butter. Then Frederick had to trick them.

One day he said to his friend, Gus. "I can write better than you can."

"No, you can't," Gus said. "I go to school. And you're only just learning."

But Frederick said again, "I can write better than you can."

"No, you can't!" Gus was getting mad.

"Yes, I can."

"Can't!"

"Can!"

Finally Gus lost his temper. "PROVE IT!" he shouted.

Frederick picked up a piece of chalk and drew all the letters he knew on a fence. Gus began to laugh. "Look!" he cried. "You've made half of them upside down!"

Frederick wanted to smile. But he kept a straight face. "All right," he said.

"Show me how to make them right side up." And Gus did.

And so, one way or another, Frederick learned. He learned until he could read and write as well as any of his friends.

But he was still a slave.

When Frederick was twelve years old he began to help one of his friends shine shoes. He didn't get much money. But he saved every penny until he had fifty cents. Then he bought a book.

It was called *THE COLUMBIAN ORATOR* — a book of stories and poems and speeches. Frederick read them all. But over and over again he returned to one — the story of a master and his slave.

The slave wanted to be free. "Prove that slavery is wrong," the master said. "Then I will set you free."

The slave argued so well he changed his master's mind. And his master set him free!

Oh, what a wonderful story that was. But that was the trouble. That's all it was

— a story in a book, and not real life.

One day Frederick sat listening to his white friends. They were unhappy because they had to mind their parents all the time. Frederick listened — and grew more and more angry. He could stand it no longer.

"You all feel so sorry for yourselves!" he burst out. "Well, *I* don't feel sorry for you. You have to mind your parents for a few years. But then you'll be grown up. Then you'll be free. I have to mind my master forever. *I am a slave for life!* Is that fair?"

"For life!" Bill exclaimed.

"It's a shame!" Joe put his hand on Frederick's shoulder.

Charley looked down at his feet.

And Gus said, "You'll be free someday, Freddy. I just *know* you will."

Frederick turned his head quickly. He didn't want his friends to see the tears in his eyes.

Fight!

THEN OLD MASTER DIED. Everything he owned was left to his family. Old Master was a rich man. He owned houses, land, money, animals. And he owned people too. By law the slaves were his property.

Frederick knew that he was more important than a piece of property. He was more important than a horse, a pig, a cow. He was a *man*. But the law said he was a slave. And now, the law said, Frederick belonged to Thomas Auld, of St. Michael's, Maryland. Thomas wrote to Hugh Auld in Baltimore, "Send me Frederick, my new slave."

Leave Baltimore? Leave his friends and his books? Leave the family he had served for so long? Frederick had lived in Baltimore since he was eight years old. Now he was sixteen. Baltimore was *home*. It was almost more than Frederick could bear. But nobody asked Frederick. In the spring of 1833 he was sent to St. Michael's — and to a different way of life.

Thomas Auld was not a kind man. He was short-tempered and stingy and mean. For the first time in seven years Frederick went hungry. For the first time in seven years he was whipped. Frederick knew he was expected to say "Yes, Master" and "No, Master" and hang his head — no matter what Thomas Auld did to him. But he could not. He could not hide the hatred in his eyes.

And Thomas Auld saw it clearly enough. "City life has ruined you!" he shouted one day. "You have forgotten how to act like a slave!"

Finally he got tired of this slave who would not bow his head, who looked at him with such cold, hard eyes. "I'm sending you to Covey's," he said. "He'll teach you some manners!"

Frederick trembled when he heard these words. He had not been in St. Michael's long. But he had been there long enough to hear of Edward Covey. Some men tamed wild horses — broke their spirits. Edward Covey broke the spirits of men.

On January 1, 1834, Frederick went to work on Mr. Covey's farm. He had never worked in the fields before. At first he was slow and clumsy. But Edward Covey thought that Frederick was just being lazy.

"Come with me," he snapped. He cut three long, thin branches from a tree. And he beat Frederick with them. When Covey was done, Frederick's back was bloody and raw. His eyes were filled with tears of pain. But "It will take more than a whipping to break *me*," he whispered.

Mr. Covey used more than whippings. He used work as well. Work, work, work . . . day and night, in all kinds of weather. No matter how hot or cold it was, the slaves had to work. It never rained, blew, hailed, or snowed enough to keep the slaves out of the fields.

Each day Frederick grew more tired. Each day it was harder to get out of bed. He never laughed or joked or thought about trying to escape anymore. Later Frederick wrote, "I was broken in body, soul, and spirit."

Then one day Mr. Covey went too far. He tried to whip Frederick once too often. Frederick clenched his fists and whirled around. No! No matter what happened he would not be whipped again!

"What?" cried Mr. Covey. His voice shook with surprise. "Are you going to fight back?"

A slave auction

"Yes, sir," Frederick answered politely. And the fight began. Some of the other slaves gathered to watch.

"Help me!" Mr. Covey cried to a slave named Bill. But Bill just shook his head and turned away. "Help me!" Mr. Covey cried to Caroline, the cook. But a new spirit seemed to have entered *all* the slaves that morning. "No," she snapped. "I won't." And she turned away too.

So on they fought alone, Frederick and Mr. Covey. One hour passed. And then two. But Mr. Covey was no longer young. And slowly he tired, until finally he gasped, "Go back to work. I would not have whipped you half so hard . . . if you had not fought back."

Frederick wanted to laugh for joy. He knew who had really won that fight! And it was much more than a fist-fight that Frederick had fought. "It was the turning point of my life as a slave," he wrote years later.

The Plan
That Failed

HE WAS A SLAVE — and he had hit a white man. This was a great crime and Frederick expected to be punished for it. He expected to be whipped, maybe even beaten to death. But weeks passed, and nothing happened.

Why? Was Mr. Covey afraid of him? Perhaps he did not want his neighbors to know he had been beaten by a sixteen-year-old boy. Whatever the reason, he did nothing. Mr. Covey never laid a hand on Frederick again.

Six months later Frederick left Mr. Covey's farm. He was sent by his master to work for another man. This man gave Frederick enough to eat and wear. Frederick no longer had to work so hard. With each passing day he grew stronger. He began to dream again.

But Frederick was tired of dreaming about freedom. It was time to act. Frederick and five other slaves decided to escape.

Frederick was their leader. He planned carefully. They would steal a boat and go as far north as they could. Then they would continue on foot through the woods. They would hide in the daytime. And they would follow the North Star at night. Frederick even wrote out passes —papers that said they were traveling on their master's business.

It was a good plan. It should have worked. But one of the slaves who was going with him grew more and more afraid. He told his master of the plan to escape. Frederick and the other slaves were arrested.

"What shall I do with my pass?" one of Frederick's friends whispered, as they marched off to jail.

"Eat it!" Frederick whispered back.

One way or another all the passes were destroyed. There was no other proof of the plan to escape. The slaves were threatened. They were whipped. But they admitted nothing. And finally they were let out of jail and sent back to work.

The slave-owners of St. Michael's did not have any proof of the runaway plot. But they had been watching Frederick. And they were very suspicious.

"I hear he's hard to whip," one said.

"I hear he can read and write."

"I hear he planned that escape . . ."

Finally the slave-owners decided that Frederick would have to leave St.

Michael's. "Get him out of here," they said to Thomas Auld. "Or we warn you, one day he'll wake up with a bullet in his head!"

Thomas Auld was very angry! Frederick had caused him nothing but trouble. "There's only one thing I can do," he said. "I'm sending you back to Baltimore."

Picking cotton

The Plan
That Did Not Fail

BALTIMORE! He was back in Baltimore again — back at the home of Hugh and Sophia Auld!

Hugh Auld got Frederick a job in a nearby shipyard. Frederick was good with his hands. Soon he was earning top wages. But every Saturday Frederick had to give all the money he earned to Master Hugh. Once in a while, when Frederick earned six dollars, Master Hugh gave Frederick back six cents.

Other blacks worked in the shipyard.

Most were slaves. But a few of them were free. They were not owned by other men. Some had been given their freedom by a kind master. Some had been born free — their parents had not been slaves. Some had been allowed to work in their free time. When they had saved up enough money, they had been allowed to buy themselves free.

Most of these free Negroes belonged to a club called "The East Baltimore Mutual Improvement Society." Once a week they got together to read and write and study. Frederick was a slave. But he could read and write. They asked him to join the club.

At one of the meetings Frederick met a girl. Her name was Anna Murray. She was tall and slim and very beautiful. "May I walk you home tonight?" Frederick asked. Anna said nothing. She was very shy. But she nodded *yes*.

Frederick walked Anna Murray home

often after that. He always had a lot to talk about. Anna was a good listener. They fell more and more in love.

Frederick's luck had certainly changed. He had a good job. He was well-treated. He was in love. But something seemed to be troubling him.

"What's the matter, honey?" Anna asked one night.

"I've got freedom on my mind," Frederick answered. He was planning again to escape.

This time Frederick decided to go alone — he had learned that it was safer this way. But he still needed help. So he turned to his friend, Stanley.

Stanley was a free Negro. He could go wherever he wanted. But he had to carry a free-paper to prove that he was not a slave. Frederick borrowed Stanley's free-paper. "I'll mail it back to you," he promised. "Just as soon as I get free."

Frederick had many close friends in

Baltimore. But he did not dare tell them of his plan. "When will I ever see them again?" Frederick wondered. He knew that the answer was probably "Never." Frederick Douglass said later that to leave his friends was the most painful decision he had to make.

As the day of escape drew near, Frederick became more and more nervous. This was his second escape attempt. It had better succeed. He might not get another.

If he were caught, Frederick knew he would be punished severely. Probably he would be sent far, far away to work on the rice and cotton plantations of Louisiana or Alabama. Escape was almost impossible from there. Later, Frederick Douglass wrote about this time in his life. He said, "It was life and death with me."

September 3, 1838, was a working day. But Frederick did not go to work. He went to Stanley's house instead. Stanley was a sailor. He gave Frederick a sailor's red shirt and a black waterproof hat. Frederick tied a sailor's kerchief around his neck. Then he went to the railroad station and climbed on a train heading north.

But he wasn't safe yet. The train was still in a slave state. What if somebody looked at the paper in his pocket too carefully? What if somebody asked him too many questions? What if somebody recognized him in spite of these sailor's clothes? Frederick had never been on a train before. He had never traveled so fast. But he whispered, *"Faster. Go faster!"*

Then it happened. The train stopped in a station. Frederick got off the train to stretch his legs. He found himself staring straight into the eyes of someone he knew.

Fred Stein was a white man. He

would know that Frederick was running away. Would he turn him in? Frederick wanted to run! He wanted to hide! But his legs felt like jelly. His feet felt like lead! All he could do was stand there — and stare.

For a long time Fred Stein stared back. Then — without a word — he turned and walked away. "He's a *good* man," Frederick thought. "He won't turn me in."

Frederick climbed back on the train. The train kept on going north, but it seemed to go so slowly! Each minute seemed like an hour. Each hour took forever to pass! Finally the train reached New York City. He jumped off.

Frederick stared up at the sky. That was *free* sky up there. He stared down at his feet. That was *free* ground he was standing on. He took a deep breath. That was *free* air he was breathing. He was free at last!

"Trust No One"

NEW YORK CITY! Frederick wanted to sing. He wanted to shout. He wanted to share his joy with someone. He looked around. New York City . . . He had never seen so many people in his life. But they were all strangers.

Then he saw a familiar face. No . . . Yes! It was an old friend, Jake! "Jake!" Frederick called. "Hey, Jake!" Once they had been as close as brothers. They had worked together in St. Michael's. They had slept under the same ragged blanket. They had shared food and jokes, secrets and dreams. Now Jake looked at Frederick — and turned away.

But it *was* Jake. Frederick was sure of it. He called again, "Jake! It's *me,* Frederick!" People were beginning to stop and stare. "Shh!" Jake whispered. And he pulled Frederick into a nearby alley.

"What are you trying to do? Get us both arrested?"

Frederick's smile faded. He didn't understand. "But Jake, this is *free* land," he said. "We're both safe here." But Jake shook his head. "Until we get caught," he said. Then he explained.

They were both runaway slaves. New York was full of slave-catchers — men who found runaways and returned them to their masters. "Trust no one," Jake said. "And get out of this town as fast as you can!"

For the next three days and nights Frederick walked around the streets of New York. He had no money, no job, no place to sleep. He grew more and more hungry, tired, and afraid.

On the fourth day Frederick saw a man watching him. The man smiled. *Trust no one,* Jake had told him. Frederick turned away.

But he couldn't go on this way much longer. He had to trust somebody soon. Frederick turned back — and the man was still there.

"Are you in trouble?" he asked.

Frederick nodded.

"Then follow me," the man said. "I'll take you to a safe place."

They walked for a long time. *Trust no one* — Frederick grew more and more afraid. "Where are you taking me?" he whispered.

"To Mr. Ruggles' house," the man answered. "He will hide you."

"Why?" Frederick wondered.

"He is an Abolitionist," the man said.

Frederick knew what this word meant. He knew that Abolitionists were men who worked to *abolish* — to end — slavery. They were friends.

"Here is his house now," the man said at last. "Good luck." And he walked away.

The door opened and Mr. Ruggles stood smiling at Frederick. Suddenly Frederick knew that everything was going to be all right. "Welcome," Mr. Ruggles said — and he pulled Frederick inside quickly.

The Speech

FREDERICK WROTE a letter, "I am safe," he wrote Anna Murray in Baltimore. "Come as fast as you can."

Anna was free. It was easy for her to join Frederick in New York. They were married in Mr. Ruggles' house. But they could not stay hidden there forever. And no other place in New York City was safe for them.

Anna and Frederick Douglass on the way to New Bedford

Where could they go? Frederick had worked in shipyards. Mr. Ruggles told him that there were many big shipyards in New Bedford, Massachusetts. Besides, the people of New Bedford were against slavery. Frederick would be much safer there.

But not safe enough. The slave-catchers were still looking for Frederick *Bailey*. Frederick *Bailey* would always be a hunted man. So Frederick would have to change his name. He changed his last name to *Douglass*.

"A new name for a new life," he told

Anna proudly. And the young couple settled down in New Bedford. By the end of the first year they had a baby daughter. Another year passed, and Frederick's first son was born.

Frederick had to work hard to support his growing family. He chopped wood, dug cellars, moved rubbish. He swept and scrubbed and loaded the big ships that sailed in and out of New Bedford harbor. He worked in a brass factory. He sawed logs in a sawmill. He took any job he could find. He worked very hard. He did not earn very much money. But Frederick didn't care. He was living as a free man at last.

But what about those who were not free? There were still almost three million slaves in the South. What about them? Frederick wanted so much to help in some way. But what could *he* do? He was only a poor runaway slave himself.

One day Frederick went to Nantucket

for a meeting of the Abolitionists — the men who were working to end slavery. All morning he listened to speeches. Then it was noon. Most of the people got up. They wandered outside to eat lunch on the lawn. They talked to the people they knew. But Frederick didn't know anyone. So he stayed in his seat.

"Mr. Douglass?" A man was standing by his side. "My name is William Coffin. I have heard you speak about slavery in New Bedford." Frederick had given a few talks at the Negro Methodist Church. "We would like you to say a few words to us here."

Talk to these important men? What could he possibly have to say to them? "I have no fine words. I have nothing to say!" Frederick said.

Mr. Coffin smiled. "But you have something better than fine words, Mr. Douglass. You have a story to tell — the story of your life as a slave."

"Will anyone be interested in that?" Frederick wondered.

Mr. Coffin nodded. And a few hours later Frederick found himself looking out at five hundred people. They were all waiting for him to begin.

Frederick was not used to giving speeches to such important men. At first he was afraid. Then the memories came rushing back. Frederick forgot to be nervous.

He talked about his mother — and how he had been taken from her. He talked about Grandmother Bailey — and how he had been taken from her, too. He talked about life at Old Master's — how hungry and cold he had been. He talked about the good days in Baltimore, and the bad days in St. Michael's. Frederick talked about his life as a slave.

When Frederick finished talking everyone in the audience stood up and cheered. A man ran up to him. His name was William Lloyd Garrison, and he was the leader of the Abolitionists. Garrison put his arm around Frederick.

"Is this a *thing* you have been listening to?" he shouted to the audience. "Is this a piece of property to be owned? Or is this a *man?*"

"A man! A man!" five hundred voices thundered back.

An Abolitionist meeting on the Boston Common

"Run, Frederick, Run"

NOW FREDERICK had a new job. The Abolitionists asked him to come to work for them. They hired him to travel around the northern states and make speeches against slavery.

Frederick's story was exciting. But he was not well known. At first only a few people came to hear him speak. One morning there were only five people in the meeting hall. Frederick began to speak anyway. But first he opened a window.

Frederick's voice was loud and clear.

It carried through the open window and into the street outside. People began to stop and listen. Many came inside. Before Frederick was finished speaking that day, the hall was packed with people.

Frederick traveled from town to town throughout the northern states. He made many friends for the Abolitionists. He made enemies too. Slavery was not allowed in the northern states. It was against the law. But many people were *prejudiced* against Negroes anyway. They thought Negroes were not as good as white people.

Frederick met this prejudice in many places. Too often he saw signs that read "No Negroes Allowed." On trains he had to ride in special cars for blacks. These cars were called "Jim Crow" cars. And they were always dirty and uncomfortable.

"Dogs and monkeys can ride first

class," one of Frederick's friends said bitterly. "But not Frederick Douglass."

On ships there was another rule. No matter how hot or cold or stormy it was, blacks had to stay out on deck, or ride below with the baggage.

One rainy night a sailor came up to him. "Are you an Indian?" he asked. Frederick knew that Indians could ride inside. He knew that all he had to say was *yes* — all he had to do was lie — and he could go inside where it was warm and dry. "No," Frederick Douglass said proudly. "I am a nigger."

Prejudice wasn't the only trouble Frederick faced in those early years as an Abolitionist speaker.

Frederick was a wonderful speaker. He could make people laugh one minute — and cry the next. But some people were beginning to say that Frederick Douglass spoke *too* well. He used too many big words, they said. Maybe he was lying. Maybe he had never been a slave at all!

"How can I prove I am telling the truth?" Frederick wondered. He could think of only one way. Frederick sat down and wrote his autobiography — the story of his life as a slave.

He told his real name — Frederick Bailey. He named the places where he had lived as a slave. He told the name of the man who still owned him — Thomas Auld.

The book was published in 1845. It was a great success. Everyone was reading it — even Thomas Auld. Now he knew where to find Frederick! He sent slave-catchers after him.

Run, Frederick, run! Hide! The slave-catchers are coming! They are coming to get you tonight!

Where could he hide? Frederick was now a famous man. He was the most wanted runaway in the United States. No place in America was safe for him. He would have to leave the country. Frederick kissed his wife. He hugged his children. And late one night he got on board a ship to England.

Many people in England had read his book. Now they came to hear him speak. For almost two years Frederick traveled across England, Scotland, Ireland, and Wales talking about the wrongs of slavery. He made many new friends.

"Send for your family and stay with us," his friends said. "You will be safe here for the rest of your life." It was true. Slavery was not allowed in England. Almost 50 years before Frederick was born, an English judge had made a rule: Any slave who set foot on English soil became a free man. But England was not his home. Frederick longed to return to America again.

Frederick's English friends wanted

him to stay with them. But even more they wanted him to be happy. So they got together and raised a great deal of money. Part of it they sent to the Aulds of Maryland to buy Frederick's freedom. Then they gave the rest of the money to him. "For the others," they said. "To help the ones who are still not free."

Frederick Douglass' "freedom paper," signed by Hugh Auld

"The Underground Railroad Is Running Tonight!"

NOW FREDERICK was free. He could go anywhere he wanted to. In the spring of 1847 he sailed back home again.

But what should he do with the money — this money for the others? Frederick had an idea — an idea that few people liked. He decided to print a newspaper so blacks could speak for themselves.

His Abolitionist friends did not think this was a good idea. Frederick had money — but not enough to run a newspaper. He had plenty of brains — but not enough education, they thought.

"You will surely fail," they told him.

Frederick listened to his friends. Then he went ahead and did what he wanted. Frederick Douglass had a great deal of confidence in himself.

He moved his family to Rochester, New York. And he began to make plans for his newspaper. But what should he call it? Frederick thought for a long time. Then he knew. When a slave planned to run away he would ask his friends how he could find his way north to free land — meaning any place where all men were free. The answer was always the same. "Just follow that old North Star in the sky. *It* will lead you to freedom." On December 3, 1847, the first copy of Frederick Douglass' newspaper, the *North Star,* came out.

The *North Star* told the true adventures of escaping slaves. It told of friends working to end slavery. It printed stories by black writers.

But Negroes were not the only people who were treated badly in America. Other groups needed help too. Women did not have equal rights with men. Poor people went hungry. Many children were forced to work long hours in dark factories. Animals were whipped to death in the streets every day. Women, children, poor people, even animals — Frederick Douglass used the *North Star* to fight for them all.

His days were crowded with work. But Frederick always found time for one more job. He always found time to work on the Underground Railroad.

The Underground Railroad was not a railroad. It had no trains. It had no tracks. But it did have *passengers* and *conductors, stations* and *station-masters.*

The runaway slaves were the passengers. The conductors were men and women who led them north. The stations were places where they rested and hid — usually the homes of people who hated slavery. These people were called station-masters.

Frederick's home in Rochester, New York, was a station on the Underground Railroad. He was its station-master. He never knew when to expect a new group of slaves. Usually they came late at night when the streets were dark and empty. A knock would sound on the door. Then Frederick and Anna would look at each other and know — *the Underground Railroad is running tonight.*

Anna would go to the kitchen to make a meal. Frederick would go to the door — but he wouldn't open it right away. First he would whisper, "Who's there?"

"*A friend with friends,*" someone would whisper back. Then Frederick knew it was safe to open the door and let the slaves slip inside. For this was the password — the secret greeting between friends on the Underground Railroad.

Frederick's whole family worked on the Railroad. His sons, Lewis, Frederick Jr., and Charles, helped him hide the slaves. They helped raise money to send them on to the next station. His daughters, Rosetta and Anna, helped their mother make the slaves comfortable. "Remember," Frederick told his family, "they are guests in our house."

They were quiet guests. They had to be. It was dangerous to travel on the Underground Railroad. The grown-ups talked in whispers. The children learned to play in whispers too. The babies were often given medicine to make them sleep. Then in September, 1850, the Underground Railroad became a lot more dangerous. For a new and terrible law was passed.

The Fugitive Slave Law said that runaway slaves *must* be returned to their masters. It also said that anyone caught hiding slaves would be fined a great deal of money or thrown into jail.

Now the slaves were not safe anywhere in the United States. Not even in the North. They had to escape to another country — to Canada. Now Frederick's house in Rochester, New York, became a very important station. For it was the last station on the line. Rochester was on one side of Lake Ontario. Across the lake lay Canada — and safety for the slaves.

The years passed and Frederick helped more than 400 slaves escape. Each time, he thought, "There goes one less slave, one more free man." The thought made his heart glad.

But sometimes Frederick grew discouraged too. He had helped hundreds to freedom. But what of the others? There were still millions of slaves in the South. What about them? Would this time of trouble never be over? Would black men never be free?

"My Job
Is Done"

FOR YEARS the people of the northern states and the people of the southern states had been arguing with each other. One of the big things they argued about was slavery. Many people began to talk about war. In April 1861, the first guns were fired. The Civil War began.

"God be praised," Frederick Douglass said when he heard the news. He knew that if the North won the war, the slaves would be free at last.

There were already many free blacks in the North. At first they were not allowed to be soldiers. They were not allowed to fight in the northern Army. "Why not?" Frederick Douglass asked over and over again. "Is this a time to fight with your *white* hand and allow your *black* hand to be tied?"

Finally blacks were allowed to become soldiers. Frederick's son Charles was the first black to enlist. His son Lewis was the second. Frederick Douglass went from city to city urging other young blacks to join the Army too.

Soon Frederick saw that black soldiers were not being treated fairly. They were paid only half as much as white soldiers. They were almost never made into officers — leaders of other men. Yet they were often sent to the most dangerous places to fight.

This made Frederick Douglass angry.

He went to Washington, D.C., to see the President. When Frederick arrived at the White House, he was very nervous. "I was born a slave," he thought. "And in a few minutes I am going to talk to the President of the United States!"

As Frederick came into the office, the President began to rise. "Goodness," Frederick thought. "I am tall — but *he* is much taller."

"Mr. President, my name is . . ." Frederick began.

The tall man smiled as he held out his hand. "I know who you are, Mr. Douglass," Abraham Lincoln said. "I know your work well. Welcome to the White House."

The two men talked for a long time. When he left the White House, Frederick Douglass thought, "That is an honest man." Abraham Lincoln liked Frederick too. And he took his advice. Soon the

President gave new orders to the Army. Black soldiers were to be treated the same as white soldiers.

The war went on. At first the South won most of the battles. But the North grew stronger and stronger. In April 1865, the last battle was fought, and the North won the war. Blacks *everywhere* were free at last.

"My job is done," Frederick Douglass said.

But was it?

This painting of Douglass as a young man hung in his study.

"Who Will Lead Us Now?"

FREDERICK DOUGLASS was forty-eight years old. He had been fighting against slavery for twenty-five years. Now, by law, Negroes were no longer slaves. Now, by law, they were full citizens of the United States. But did they have true freedom? Did they have the right to live and work as free men? Most of them had no money, no education, no land. There was still prejudice against them almost everywhere.

In many places blacks were not allowed to go into theaters or hotels or churches. They had to ride at the back of streetcars. When they rode on trains they had to ride in special cars.

In many places blacks were not allowed to be postmen or firemen or lawyers or doctors. They were allowed to do only the hard work, the dirty work no one else wanted to do.

True, the law said that blacks now had the right to vote. But most of them did not dare to use the right. In many places there were white men who did not want black men to be free. Mobs of these white men rode through the night to frighten blacks. They set fires and burned homes. And each year they murdered hundreds.

"But who cares?" one black newspaperman wrote.

"*I* care," Frederick Douglass said.

He was a successful man. He had many

important jobs. Presidents and senators and judges asked his advice. He was one of the most famous men in America. It would have been easy for him to say that he had done enough. It would have been easy for him to forget the others who still needed help. But he did not.

For the rest of his long life Frederick Douglass fought for laws that would protect his people. He fought for better schools for the children, better jobs for the men. He fought for the day when the signs would come down everywhere — the signs that said: "No Negroes Allowed."

"Go slow, Douglass," his friends warned. "These are dangerous times. You will get hurt if you're not careful."

"I won't go slow," Frederick snapped. "The only way you get something is to *fight* for it."

So the years passed and he kept fighting. Frederick Douglass lived to be

seventy-eight years old. Sometimes he grew tired of traveling, of talking, of fighting. But there was always one more battle to win — and so little time left.

Then there was none. It was February 20, 1895. He had fought his last fight.

It was raining on the day of Frederick Douglass' funeral. But early in the morning people began to gather at the church — The Metropolitan African Methodist Episcopal Church in Washington, D.C. The church was soon filled. And still more came until 25,000 people stood in the rain outside.

Many were white. Some were rich and famous. But most were poor and black. Some were crying. Some stood sad and silent. Then a woman turned to her husband and said what was in the hearts of so many. "Who will lead us now that Frederick Douglass is gone?"

All across America people were asking this question. But many others remembered that Frederick Douglass had written not long before he died, "Others will fight on."

He had faith that others would fight

on until the last bit of prejudice was gone — until people everywhere understood that "One man's skin can be black and another man's skin can be white — but *under* the skin we are all the same."

Douglass' home in Washington is now the Frederick Douglass Institute of Negro Arts and Letters.